Jul Caesar

A Shakespeare Story

RETOLD BY ANDREW MATTHEWS
ILLUSTRATED BY TONY ROSS

ORCHARD

For Stephen
A.M.

ORCHARD BOOKS
338 Euston Road, London NW1 3BH
Orchard Books Australia
Hachette Children's Books
Level 17/207 Kent St, Sydney, NSW 2000
First published in Great Britain in 2009
First paperback publication in 2010
This slipcase edition published in 2013
Not for individual resale
Text © Andrew Matthews 2009
Illustrations © Tony Ross 2009
ISBN 978 1 40780 978 6
The rights of Andrew Matthews to be identified as the author and Tony Ross as
the illustrator of this work have been asserted by them in accordance with the
Copyright, Designs and Patents Act, 1988.
A CIP catalogue record for this book is available from the British Library
Printed in China

Orchard Books is a division of Hachette Childrens Books,
an Hachette UK company.
www.hachette.co.uk

Contents

Cast List

Julius Caesar

Victorious Roman general,
and senator

Mark Antony

Close friend of Caesar

Brutus

Well-respected nobleman

Cassius

Brilliant general, and
conspirator against Caesar

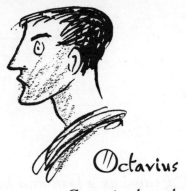

Octavius

Caesar's adopted son

Dessius

Roman nobleman,
and conspirator against Caesar

Strato

Servant to Brutus

The Scene

Rome, 44BC

Yond Cassius has a lean and hungry look,
He thinks too much; such men are dangerous.

Caesar; I.ii.

Julius Caesar

The streets of Rome were lined with bustling crowds. They had gathered to honour Julius Caesar, Rome's most brilliant general. Caesar had led his armies

to victory after victory, and the Roman
Republic had grown in size and wealth.
To show their gratitude, the citizens of
Rome had elected Caesar as their Consul.

When Caesar appeared, mounted on a
fine white horse, the crowds called out his

name, and threw handfuls of flower petals that drifted through the air like coloured snow. Caesar stared straight ahead, and did not wave or smile. With his hooked nose and hooded eyes, he looked as proud and cruel as an eagle.

Suddenly, an old man ran out into the road. Caesar struggled for a moment to calm his startled horse, and then glared coldly. The crowds stopped cheering, and the only sound was the jingling harness of Caesar's horse.

"What do you want, old man?" Caesar demanded.

"Caesar!" the old man cried hoarsely. "Beware the Ides of March!"

Caesar scowled, but then his lips stretched into a mocking smile. "Stand aside!" he said sternly. "I am Caesar. I fear nothing and no one."

When they heard these words, the crowds roared their approval – but not everyone cheered. From the steps of a nearby temple, two Roman noblemen were watching Caesar, and they frowned at what they saw.

One of the men was thin and restless. Envy burned in his eyes as he spoke.

"Look how the people love him, Brutus!" he said. "I think it won't be long before they make Caesar their king!"

The other man nodded gravely. "I'm afraid you may be right, Cassius," he agreed, "and I'm also afraid of the kind of king Caesar would be."

"Afraid?" said Cassius.

"Caesar's pride grows with his power," Brutus said. "I fear that if he becomes king, he'll be a tyrant, and the people of Rome will be no better than his slaves."

"Then he must be stopped," Cassius said softly.

Brutus gave his companion a sharp glance. "How?" he said.

Cassius said
nothing, but his
right hand
tapped the hilt
of the dagger
at his side.

"Who would
dare to raise a
hand against
Caesar?" said
Brutus. "The
people would riot!"

"I know a group of noblemen who
would kill Caesar if they were led by a
man they could trust," said Cassius. "A
man so respected that the people would
listen to him when he explained the
reasons why Caesar had to die. A man
like you, Brutus."

Brutus stood deep in thought for a while, then he said, "Who are these nobles?"

"Myself, of course," Cassius told him, "Casca, Decius, Metellus and Trebonius."

"Give me time to consider the matter," said Brutus.

"There is a time to think and a time for action, Brutus," Cassius warned. "Don't wait until it's too late."

Brutus pondered long and hard. He had been a loyal friend of Caesar's, but he knew that power had made Caesar ruthless.

He's like a deadly snake inside its shell, Brutus thought. *If he isn't killed before he hatches, he'll poison all Rome. But could I really bring myself to kill a friend?*

On the day before the Ides of March, Cassius brought Brutus alarming news.

"Caesar will go to the Senate tomorrow morning," Cassius said. "The Senate means to offer him a royal crown."

Brutus gave a loud sigh, and ran his left hand through his hair. "Then my darkest nightmares are coming true!" he groaned.

"Join us, Brutus!" Cassius urged. "Together we can stop Caesar, and save Rome."

Brutus's face was deathly pale, and he spoke in a voice that was no more than a whisper. "Send a message to the others," he said. "Tell them to meet at my house at midnight. Say that I will lead them to do what must be done."

* * *

That night, the conspirators met in the orchard of Brutus's garden, far from spying eyes and ears. Brutus greeted them, then said, "When Caesar goes to the Senate House tomorrow, we will meet him

there, and listen while Metellus begs forgiveness for his banished brother. If Caesar is not merciful, we will strike him down."

"Will Caesar be the only one to die?" asked Metellus. "What about Mark Antony? Caesar treats him like a son. He's bound to be against us."

"Metellus is right!" said Cassius. "Let Caesar and Mark Antony die together."

"No, Cassius," Brutus said. "We're not butchers! If we spare Mark Antony, it will show that we're not acting out of jealousy or spite, but for the good of Rome."

Cassius wondered if this were wise, but he kept his doubts to himself. "As you wish, Brutus," he said.

* * *

Early next morning, Decius, one of the conspirators, arrived at Caesar's villa in order to accompany him to the Senate House. He was bewildered and dismayed when Caesar informed him that he intended to cancel the visit.

"Should I tell the Senators that you have been taken ill, mighty Caesar?" Decius enquired. "I will not stoop to lying," replied Caesar. "Just tell them that I do not wish to come."

"But I will be laughed at if I do not give a reason for your absence!" Decius cried. Caesar's face went red with fury. "I am Caesar! I do not have to make excuses to the Senate for what I do!"

But his anger vanished as swiftly as it had
appeared, and he spoke more calmly.
"However, since you are a good friend,
Decius, I shall tell you the truth. Last
night, my wife Calpurnia dreamed that a
huge statue of me stood in the Forum.
The statue began to gush out fountains of
blood. Many citizens washed their hands
in the blood, and smiled as they did so.

Calpurnia believes that the dream was sent to her by the gods, to warn me that I will be in danger if I go out today. She has persuaded me to stay at home."

Decius thought frantically. If Caesar did not go to the Senate House, the conspirators' plot would fail. Suddenly, a solution came to him.

"Great Caesar, Calpurnia misunderstood her dream!" he insisted smoothly. "The Gods meant it as a sign that you will bring new life to Rome. That is why the citizens smiled in gratitude as they bathed in your blood."

Caesar stroked his chin. "Your reading of Calpurnia's dream is interesting, Decius," he murmured.

"I can prove I am right!" Decius declared. "I know that the Senators are planning to make you the King of Rome today. If you do not go to the Senate, they might change their minds. Or should I tell them they must wait until Calpurnia has better dreams? They will mock you, and say you are a coward."

Decius's words stung Caesar's pride. "Who dares to call Caesar a coward?" he growled. "Cowards imagine a thousand different deaths for themselves. Brave men only die once. Very well, Decius! Let us go to the Senate. On the way, I will decide whether to accept the Senators' offer of a crown."

Caesar's route to the Senate House was lined with cheering citizens. As he mounted the steps of the building, Caesar wore a triumphant smile, but the smile was replaced by a frown of

irritation when he saw a group of nobles, including Brutus and Cassius, blocking the doorway. "What is the meaning of this?" Caesar snapped.

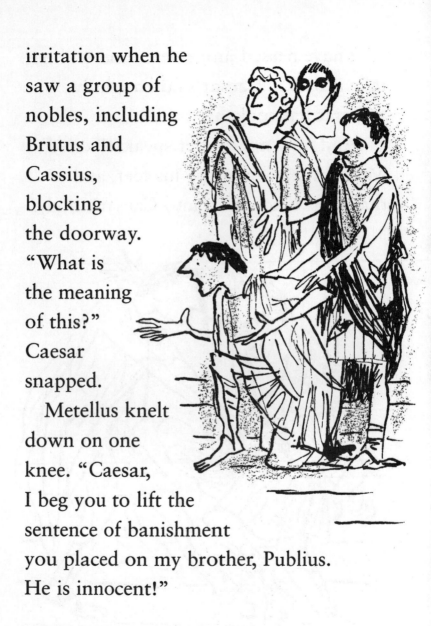

Metellus knelt down on one knee. "Caesar, I beg you to lift the sentence of banishment you placed on my brother, Publius. He is innocent!"

"I have passed judgement, and will not take it back," Caesar said haughtily. "Caesar has spoken!"

"And now my dagger speaks!" cried Metellus. He sprang to his feet, and thrust his blade deep into Caesar's body.

The other conspirators were quick to follow. The last to strike was Brutus, and when he pulled his dagger out of Caesar, Caesar staggered against him.

"What, you too, Brutus?" Caesar gasped, then fell dead at Brutus's feet.

The air was shrill with shouts and screams. The crowds ran, scattering in all directions like the broken pieces of a shattered glass. A stream of Senators poured out of the Senate House. Some stared at Caesar in silent horror, others fled in fear of their lives.

Only Brutus remained calm. He stooped, and pressed his palms into the red pool that was spreading around Caesar's body, then lifted his hands high for all to see. "Peace!" he called. "Freedom! Liberty!"

At that moment, Mark Antony appeared. The morning sun shone on his fair curly hair as he walked up to Brutus. Mark Antony pulled open his toga, and offered Brutus his bare chest. "If you mean to kill me, Brutus, do it now!" he said boldly.

"Live, and be our friend, Mark Antony!" Brutus pleaded. "Join us in the making of a new Rome."

Mark Antony closed his toga, and hung his head in grief. "All I ask is to be allowed to take Caesar's body to the Market Place, and say a few words in his memory," he said.

"Of course," said Brutus.

Cassius drew Brutus aside. "Have you lost your wits, Brutus?" he hissed. 'Mark Antony is one of the greatest public speakers in Rome! If he stirs up the people—"

"I'll go with him, and speak first," Brutus interrupted. "Once I've made the people understand why Caesar had to die, Mark Antony will not dare to say a word against us."

Cassius held his tongue, but once more he wondered if Brutus were doing the right thing. Brutus was a great speaker and was able to make people see common sense; but Mark Antony could move people's hearts with his words.

* * *

The Market Place was lit by flickering
torches that sent black smoke twisting
into the evening air.

A jostling crowd had assembled, but
the people stood aside to make way
for Brutus.

Mark Antony was close behind him, following two soldiers who carried the stretcher on which Caesar had been laid, covered with a white sheet.

When Brutus reached the middle of the
square, the crowd formed a circle around
him. Some stood on the backs of carts to
get a better view. Everybody knew that
something important had happened, but
nobody was sure why – they hoped that

Brutus would be able to explain, as he had explained so often in the past.

"Fellow citizens!" Brutus began. 'You know me as a man of honour. I respected Caesar as much as anyone here, and I loved him as a friend – but he had grown too powerful. He became cruel and ruthless, and he would have been a tyrant if he had been made king. It would have meant the end of freedom in Rome. I stabbed Caesar so that you, and your children, and your children's children, would have liberty, not slavery."

Brutus lifted his dagger with a bloodstained hand, and the blade gleamed crimson in the torchlight. "This is the dagger I used on Caesar!" he declared. "I will use it on myself now, if the Roman people wish me to."

A voice from the crowd called out, "No! Live, Brutus! Live!" More voices joined it, until it seemed that the whole Market Place was chanting Brutus's name.

Brutus held up his hand for quiet, and when it came, he said, "I must leave you now, but I have given Mark Antony permission to speak. Stay, and listen to him."

"He'd better not say anything against Brutus!" someone shouted.

"Brutus killed his best friend to give us liberty!" said someone else.

Mark Antony waited with his head bowed until Brutus had left the Market Place, then he showed his face, and peered at the crowd. "Friends! Romans! Countrymen! Lend me your ears!" he begged. "I haven't come here to try to turn you against Brutus, but to say goodbye to my friend, Julius Caesar.

Noble Brutus has said that
Caesar was cruel and
ruthless – and Brutus
would not lie to
you! He is a man
of honour. See
here, on
Caesar's corpse,
the wound that
the honourable
Brutus made
when he
stabbed his
dearest friend
through the
heart!"

Mark Antony
pulled back the cloth
covering Caesar, and the crowd gasped.

As they stared at the bloody corpse,
with its wounds gaping like red mouths,
Mark Antony drew a parchment from the
folds of his toga. "This is Caesar's will!"
he announced. "He has left all his palaces
and gardens to the people of Rome. His
fortune will be shared out, and every
citizen will be given five pieces of silver.

Is this the will of a cruel
and ruthless man?
Would a tyrant
do this?"

"No!" the
crowd replied
angrily.

"Calm
yourselves, my
friends!" said
Mark Antony.
"Or you might start
to think that Caesar was a
more honourable man than Brutus!"

"Brutus is a villain!" someone shouted.
"Let's drive the men who murdered
Caesar out of the city."

With a great bellow, the crowd surged
off in the direction that Brutus had taken.

"Now great Caesar will be avenged!"
Mark Antony murmured to himself.

That night, a riot spread across Rome.
The homes of the conspirators were
looted and set on fire. For many days
there was fighting in the streets, and the
conflict rapidly boiled over into civil war.

Mark Antony and Octavius, Caesar's nephew, took command of the Roman army, and gained control of the city. They swore to hunt down all the conspirators and put them to death.

Brutus and Cassius escaped from Rome, and raised an army of loyal supporters. They drew up their forces on a wide plain near a small town, and there they waited.

It was not long before the army of
Mark Antony and Octavius found them.

From a hill above their camp, Cassius watched the enemy troops advance in two wide columns, marching to the throb of drums and the blaring of brass horns. Sunlight glittered on bronze breastplates and the tips of spears.

"This may be the last time we meet,
so farewell, Cassius," Brutus said,
grasping Cassius's hand.

"Farewell, my friend," said Cassius.
"If we do meet again, we'll smile
about this moment over a cup of wine.
If not..." He shrugged and walked
away.

The armies clashed, and for a long time there was noise and confusion. But by late afternoon, the outcome of the battle was clear: Brutus and Cassius had been defeated. Cassius died fighting, and when they learned of his death, the last of his troops gave up hope and fled.

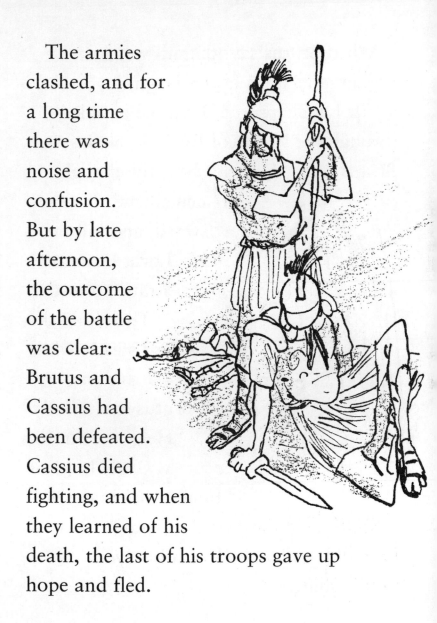

When Brutus saw that all was lost, he summoned his faithful captain, Strato.

"If I am captured, I will be paraded through the streets of Rome in chains," Brutus said. "I cannot bear the thought of such shame. Take my sword, and kill me."

"My Lord, I cannot!" Strato protested.

"Then hold the sword steady while I run onto it," Brutus said calmly. "Help me, Strato. My only hope of honour lies in death."

Strato held the sword as straight as he could, and waited with his eyes tightly shut.

When Brutus's body was brought before Octavius and Mark Antony, Octavius was surprised to see tears in Mark Antony's eyes. "You should rejoice," Octavius said. "Our enemy is dead."

"He was the noblest of us all, Octavius," said Mark Antony. "The others killed Caesar because they were jealous of his power. Brutus only did what he believed was right. Now Brutus and Caesar are gone, and Rome will never see such greatness again."

The two men stared at each other in the red light of sunset, and wondered what kind of victory it was that they had won.

This was the noblest Roman of them all

Anthony; V.v.

Liberty and Power in Julius Ceasar

Shakespeare wrote *Julius Caesar* in 1599. He took the story from Sir Thomas North's translation of *Lives* by the Ancient Greek writer, Plutarch.

Writing about rulers being overthrown was a risky business in Shakespeare's time, and he handles the subject with great care.

Julius Caesar is shown as an arrogant character. Power has made him dismissive of other people, and, if made king, he might well become the tyrant that Brutus fears. On the other hand, his murder is both brutal and cruel.

Brutus is a man of principle, who acts from the highest motives. He kills his friend because he believes that if he does not, the freedom of Rome's citizens will be at risk. Brutus is convinced that other people are as moved by common sense as he is himself. He is proven tragically wrong.

Mark Antony is a skilful manipulator who understands that the common people of Rome think with their hearts, not their heads. He at first hides his anger towards the conspirators, because he knows that if he lets his true feelings show, he will be killed. His speech in the Market Place is a masterpiece of double meaning. Each time he uses the word "honourable" he makes his audience question exactly how honourable Brutus is.

The conspirators' violent action has violent consequences. The country is plunged into the chaos of civil war. Shakespeare shows us that in the world of politics, assassination can turn against those who employ it. It is ironic that Brutus, who intends to protect Roman liberty, starts a chain of events that eventually leads to Rome being ruled by a long line of ruthless dictators – the emperors.

Shakespeare and the Globe Theatre

Some of Shakespeare's most famous plays were first performed at the Globe Theatre, which was built on the South Bank of the River Thames in 1599.

Going to the Globe was a different experience from going to the theatre today. The building was roughly circular in shape, but with flat sides: a little like a doughnut crossed with a fifty-pence piece. Because the Globe was an open-air theatre, plays were only put on during daylight hours in spring and summer. People paid a penny to stand in the central space and watch a play, and this part of the audience became known as 'the groundlings' because they stood on the ground. A place in the tiers of seating beneath the thatched roof, where there was a slightly better view and less chance of being rained on, cost extra.

The Elizabethans did not bath very often and the audiences at the Globe were smelly. Fine ladies and gentlemen in the more expensive seats sniffed perfume and bags of sweetly scented herbs to cover the stink rising from the groundlings.

There were no actresses on the stage; all the female characters in Shakespeare's plays would have been acted by boys, wearing wigs and make-up. Audiences were not well behaved. People clapped and cheered when their favourite actors came on stage; bad actors were jeered at and sometimes pelted with whatever came to hand.

Most Londoners worked hard to make a living and in their precious free time they liked to be entertained. Shakespeare understood the magic of the theatre so well that today, almost four hundred years after his death, his plays still cast a spell over the thousands of people that go to see them.

Orchard Classics
Shakespeare Stories

RETOLD BY ANDREW MATTHEWS
ILLUSTRATED BY TONY ROSS

Orchard Books are available from all good bookshops.